At Sunset

Becca Heddle

Contents

Explorer Challenge

Who rests upside down?

OXFORD

UNIVERSITY PRESS

A lot happens at sunset.

It gets dark as the sun sets.

I go to the burrow at sunset.

I go to hunt rats at sunset.

I go back to the burrow at sunset.

At Sunset

Look Back, Explorers

Where does the owl go at sunset?

Can you point to an animal that goes to a burrow at sunset?

What does the word *sunset* mean?

Did you find out who rests upside down?

Explorer Challenge: the butterfly (pages 6 and 10)

What's Next, Explorers?

Now join Biff, Chip and Kipper on a picnic at sunset ...

Explorer Challenge
for *A Picnic at Sunset*

What is Chip pointing at?